WALL PILATES

WORKOUTS FOR WOMEN

KRISTEN PAYTON

TABLE OF CONTENTS

HOW TO DOWNLOAD YOUR BONUSES:

- VIDEO COURSE WITH 80 STEP BY STEP VIDEOS
- 40 EXTRA EXERCISES
- 30 DAY CHALLENGE EXTRA

WALL PILATES INTRODUCTION
- A REVOLUTION IN THE WORLD OF FITNESS
- WHY THIS BOOK IS DIFFERENT
- HOW TO KEEP YOUR MOTIVATION HIGH
- HOW TO AVOID COMMON MISTAKES

EXERCISES

DOWNLOAD ALL THE BONUSES HERE IN A FEW SECONDS AND START PRACTICING WALL PILATES NOW!

Are you ready to start a new sporting discipline that will transform you in no time?

I thank you with affection for choosing to purchase this amazing book full of informative content and practical exercises that you can replicate comfortably at home at any time. We have dedicated a lot of time, passion, and energy to ensure we create a UNIQUE COMPREHENSIVE GUIDE that includes:

- THEORETICAL INTRODUCTION
- 40 EXERCISES WITH TEXTUAL EXPLANATION AND STEP BY STEP PHOTOS
- 30 DAY TRAINING PROGRAM

As promised, however, this is not all... we have included the following BONUSES:

1st BONUS: 40 VIDEO RECORDINGS OF THE EXERCISES PRESENT INSIDE THE BOOK

2nd BONUS: 40 MORE MEDIUM - ADVANCED EXERCISES WITH RELATED VIDEOS

3rd BONUS: AN ADDITIONAL 30 DAY ADVANCED TRAINING PROGRAM

**Purchasing this book, you will have totally free access to:**

1 - MAIN THEORETICAL NOTIONS ON WALL PILATES

2 - 40 BASIC AND INTERMEDIATE EXERCISES WITH:

- TEXTUAL EXPLANATION

- STEP BY STEP ILLUSTRATIONS

- 30 DAY TRAINING PROGRAM

- VIDEO RECORDINGS

3 - 40 MEDIUM-ADVANCED EXERCISES WITH:

- TEXTUAL EXPLANATION

- STEP BY STEP ILLUSTRATIONS

- 30 DAY ADVANCED TRAINING PROGRAM

- VIDEO RECORDINGS

HOW TO DOWNLOAD YOUR BONUSES:

WRITE AN EMAIL TO:
wallpilates.bonus@gmail.com

WALL PILATES INTRODUCTION

A REVOLUTION IN THE WORLD OF FITNESS

This book is entirely dedicated to wall Pilates, inside you will find a complete guide perfect for you who want to start practicing this new activity in the fitness panorama. Pilates is a type of exercise that focuses on the abdomen and improves mobility, flexibility and above all posture.

But what makes it so special when performed on the wall?

Traditional Pilates, invented by Joseph Pilates, has always aimed at finding harmony between mind and body, the introduction of the wall as a "tool" has made this activity even more interesting. The use of the wall, in fact, allows you to perform a greater variety of exercises, diversifying your training routine. In fact, it is possible to carry out both challenging exercises and simpler exercises suitable for beginners. The advantage of wall Pilates consists in the active involvement of multiple muscles of the body at the same time, in fact, each movement requires coordination, balance, and strength. The use of the wall therefore allows the creation of complete and diversified training plans, guaranteeing stimulation of all areas of the body. Nonetheless, some exercises are more specific and involve only specific areas of the body to strengthen and tone them. In general, however, all exercises involve the stabilizer muscles and the abdominals; in fact, to perform each movement as best as possible it is necessary to have good coordination and good balance. The exercises in the book aim not only to tone and strengthen the body's muscles but also to improve posture and breathing. This discipline is also flexible, whether you are a high-level athlete or a beginner just starting out, the exercises can be adapted to your needs and abilities. This book will guide you through a transformation journey your body and your mind.

WHY THIS BOOK IS DIFFERENT

The world of fitness is constantly evolving, in fact, new trends and training methodologies regularly emerge that promise immediate and effortless body transformations.

So how do you identify what really works?

Wall Pilates is certainly a discipline that combines tradition and innovation, it is not a passing fad, in fact, it has proven to be a revolutionary practice in the world of fitness. Many people practice it every day and share their results and improvements with utmost transparency.

Do you want to start your body and mental transformation too?

This book is your ultimate guide that you will need to consult regularly and follow step by step. Below you will find a list of all the main features of this book that make it different from others:

Based on Real Experience

This book contains a training program tested several times on many people, it is therefore not based on abstract theories but on real experiences. The woman who performs the exercises in the videos, in fact, is following all the advice of the program to the letter and is achieving extraordinary results.

Each exercise was recorded on video

Most other books consist of a brief textual explanation and a few stylized depictions of the movement to be performed. How do you understand and distinguish exactly the movement of an exercise without seeing a person performing it?
This book includes video recordings of each exercise that enrich and contextualize the textual information and images. This way, you will be able to fully understand the movement and repeat it without any doubt with no risk of injury due to incorrect execution.

Suitable for all levels

Inside the book you will find many exercises, some of these will be simple while others a little more difficult. Everyone is unique and starts from a different physical condition, this book was in fact written with the goal of being inclusive and adaptable. Whether you are a complete beginner or a fitness veteran, you will find advice, modifications, and variations to adjust the exercises to your needs.

Variety of exercises

The exercises contained within this guide have been chosen carefully and logically to offer a variety of options and movements so as to involve all the muscles of the body.

This book, therefore, is not just one of the many Pilates manuals you can find on the internet, but is a complete guide, designed to accompany you at every stage of your journey, offering tools, advice, and support to help you achieve the best version of yourself.

HOW TO KEEP YOUR MOTIVATION HIGH

To achieve any type of goal you need to always stay motivated, be consistent and commit seriously to what you are doing. In particular, when it comes to wall Pilates, maintaining high motivation is the key to seeing real progress and truly achieving the body condition you so desire. The motivation varies over time, however, the right strategies and a proactive approach, can help you maintain a high level of motivation, ensuring your wall Pilates practice remains rewarding and productive.

In this section, you will find a series of strategies and suggestions to stay motivated over time:

1. Remember Your "Why":

Each person who purchased this book has a different "why", many approached wall Pilates because they were looking for a discipline, they could do comfortably at home to improve their health and physical condition. Others, however, already engage in another sport activity and want to learn how to perform Pilates exercises on the wall to improve mental well-being. The reasons are various, I advise you to write your "why" on a piece of paper and hang it on the wall that you will use to carry out the exercises. When your motivation drops, you can always read it and remind yourself why you started and what your goal is.

2. Set clear and measurable goals:

It is essential to set clear and measurable goals to track changes and have a clear direction to follow. I advise you to set short- and long-term goals. This will allow you to celebrate small successes and increase your motivation and self-confidence.

3. Create a Routine:

It's essential to have a routine and follow it carefully, choose specific days and times to dedicate to training, and stick to them as you would with any other significant commitment. Just this way you will obtain tangible results even in a short time.

4. Vary your training

There will be times when you start to get bored and feel the exercises are monotonous. Rather than skipping training, you may want to try new exercises or change the environment in which you perform them. You can also help yourself by listening to your favourite music or doing workouts with another person.

5. Celebrate your successes:

Recognizing and celebrating your successes, even the smallest ones, can be a powerful source of motivation. Share your achievements with friends or family and keep them updated on your progress. You can also purchase a small diary to record your progress. I also recommend that you periodically review your goals and adapt your routine taking into account your progress. Take time each month to reflect on your improvements, strengths, and weaknesses.

HOW TO AVOID COMMON MISTAKES

Every person who starts a new business makes mistakes, but it is vital to identify the most common mistakes to try to avoid them right away. These mistakes can increase the risk of injury or lead to frustration. Wall Pilates is not a risky discipline, however, like any form of exercise, it is essential to pay close attention to the execution of the exercises (I advise you to download the videos immediately!) to avoid unpleasant injuries. Below I have listed some of the most common mistakes to unequivocally avoid:

1. Skipping the warm-up:

Warming up is essential before every workout. Take 5-10 minutes to warm up your body and activate your muscles. Skipping the warm-up significantly increases the risk of injury. Before each workout, perform basic static and dynamic stretching exercises and don't forget to include basic movements to activate the muscles.

2. Incorrect execution of exercises

To limit the risk of injury it is necessary to understand the entire movement to be performed for each exercise. By purchasing this book, you have free access to all videos of all exercises, this way you will minimize the possibility of hurting yourself during training. In fact, incorrect execution not only reduces the effectiveness of the exercise but can lead to injuries and block your training program. Download the exercise videos now before continuing reading.

3. Having unrealistic expectations:

No sporting activity can guarantee immediate and effortless results. It is important to recognize that progress and change take time, consistency, and dedication. Don't set unrealistic goals and try to enjoy the journey by celebrating even the small successes. Having overly ambitious expectations can lead to frustration and discouragement.

4. Neglecting breathing:

Breathing is a fundamental component of Pilates, it helps to improve concentration and get the maximum benefit from each exercise. Make sure you pay attention to your breathing techniques as well as your execution of the exercise.

5. Don't listen to your body:

Ignoring your body's signals, such as pain or fatigue, can lead to injury or overtraining. If you feel pain or excessive fatigue, take a break, or adapt the exercise. Wall Pilates should test and challenge you, but you should never overdo it. Listen to your body and focus on performing the exercise especially at the beginning.

1 - FORWARD BEND FROM A SEATED POSITION

This exercise will improve the mobility of your lower and upper back while also stretching your calves and hamstrings.

STEP BY STEP EXECUTION

1 sit on the mat keeping your back straight and leaning against the wall

2 stretch your legs

3 keep your arms straight and place your hands on your knees

4 bend forward until your hands touch your toes

5 hold the position for 2-3 seconds

6 ascend slowly with arms outstretched

7 repeat the movement

TIPS ON HOW BEST TO CARRY OUT THE EXERCISE

The first few times you may need to bend your knees slightly to be able to touch your feet.

Inhale when you are in the starting position and exhale when you stretch.

2 - KNEES TO CHEST WHEN SEATED

This exercise will activate the hip flexor muscles and improve the joint mobility of the legs.

STEP BY STEP EXECUTION

1 it on the mat keeping your back straight and leaning against the wall

2 extend your arms at your sides and place your hands on the floor

3 stretch your legs

4 bring your right knee towards your chest, sliding your heel to the floor

5 hold the position for a second

6 return to the starting position with straight legs and do the same movement with the other leg

TIPS ON HOW BEST TO CARRY OUT THE EXERCISE

Never remove your back from the wall to get closer to your knee, try to move only your legs and keep your torso still, helping yourself with your hands which must remain fixed on the floor.

While performing the exercise, maintain regular and constant breathing.

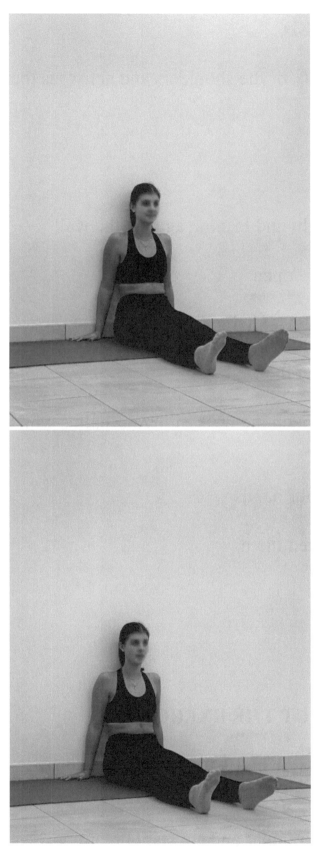
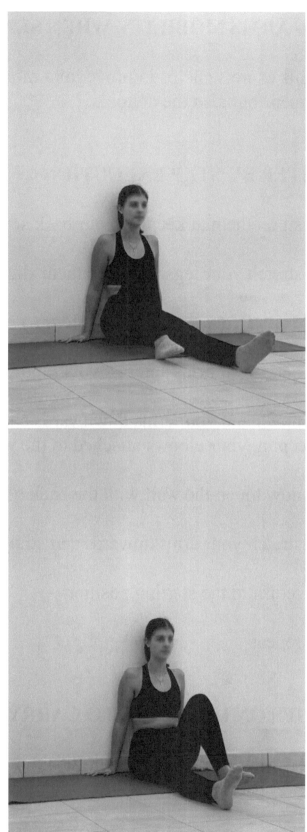

3 - ARMS MOBILITY WHEN SEATED

This exercise helps improve joint mobility of the shoulders and activates the triceps but also the deltoids.

STEP BY STEP EXECUTION

1 sit on the mat keeping your back straight and leaning against the wall

2 stretch your legs and keep them slightly open

3 extend your arms in front of you at shoulder height

4 bend your arms and rest your elbows on the wall

5 now bend your arms downwards and touch the wall with your palms while keeping your elbows attached to the wall

6 now touch the wall with the back of your hands

7 stretch your arms upwards and straighten them

8 return to the starting position

9 repeat

TIPS ON HOW BEST TO CARRY OUT THE EXERCISE

Perform the movement calmly without haste and without rounding your lower back.

While performing the exercise, maintain regular and constant breathing.

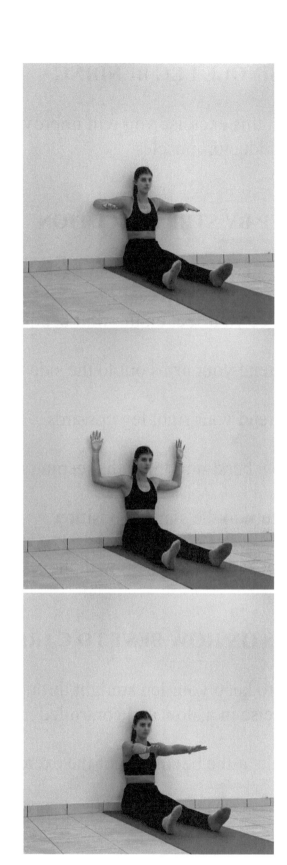

6

4 - SINGLE LEG BENDING

With this exercise you will improve the mobility of the hips by also involving the adductor muscles.

STEP BY STEP EXECUTION

1 lie on the floor with your back resting on the floor

2 place your feet on the wall bending your knees at 90 degrees

3 extend your arms out to the side with palms facing down

4 extend your right leg upwards

5 now bend it to the right keeping it taut

6 return to the starting position

7 repeat the movement with the left leg

TIPS ON HOW BEST TO CARRY OUT THE EXERCISE

Try to keep your leg straight throughout the movement and perform the exercise in a slow and controlled manner.

Inhale at the beginning of the exercise and exhale slowly as you bend your leg.

5 - ARM STRETCHING

This movement will stretch your laterals abs and activate your oblique abdominals.

STEP BY STEP EXECUTION:

1 stand up with your back and glutes leaning against the wall

2 extend your arms at your sides

3 raise your right arm keeping it attached to the wall

4 stretch the abdomen well

5 return to the starting position

6 do the same with your left arm

TIPS ON HOW BEST TO CARRY OUT THE EXERCISE

Keep your arms as straight as possible throughout the movement and perform exercise calmly and with concentration.

While performing the exercise, maintain regular and constant breathing.

6 - SINGLE-LEG LATERAL SWING

This movement improves hip mobility and balance.

STEP BY STEP EXECUTION

1 stand up with your hands resting on the wall

2 move your right leg sideways in a controlled manner

3 keep your left leg straight

4 do the same with the left leg

TIPS FOR PERFORMING THE EXERCISE BEST:

Don't move your leg too quickly and maintain balance throughout the execution.

While performing the exercise, maintain regular and constant breathing.

7 - STRETCHING INVERSE FROG POSITION

Excellent static exercise to stretch the adductor muscles.

STEP BY STEP EXECUTION:

1 lie down with your back resting on the floor

2 place your feet on the wall by bending your legs at 90 degrees

3 spread your legs and touch the wall with your feet

4 stretch your arms

5 hold the position (follow the instructions in the program)

TIPS FOR PERFORMING THE EXERCISE BEST:

Relax your legs and back while performing.

While performing the exercise, maintain regular and constant breathing.

8 - CALF STRETCH

This exercise is ideal for relaxing and stretching your calf muscles.

STEP BY STEP EXECUTION

1 stand up with your hands resting on the wall

2 bring your left leg forward and touch the wall with the toes of your left foot

3 extend your right leg backwards and keep it straight

4 bend your left leg until your knee touches the wall

5 return to starting position and repeat (follow directions in the program)

6 then repeat with the right leg

TIPS ON HOW BEST TO CARRY OUT THE EXERCISE

To improve the effectiveness of the exercise, bring your right foot as far back as possible.

While performing the exercise, maintain regular and constant breathing.

9 - ONE-SIDED WALL SLIDING

This movement will improve hip flexibility and activate your flexors.

STEP BY STEP EXECUTION

1 lie down with your back and arms resting on the floor

2 stretch your legs and place your heels on the wall

3 slide your left foot on the wall bringing your knee towards you

4 do not remove your feet from the wall during the movement

5 return to the starting position

6 repeat with the other leg

TIPS FOR PERFORMING THE EXERCISE BEST:

Extend your arms and keep them at shoulder height to maintain balance.

Inhale when you are in the starting position and exhale when you begin to bend your leg.

10 - LYING DOWN WALK

Excellent exercise ideal for activating the hip joint.

STEP BY STEP EXECUTION

1 lie on the floor with your back resting on the floor

2 extend your arms at your sides

3 stretch your legs and place your heels on the wall

4 bend your right leg and place the entire sole of your foot on the wall

5 do the same with the left leg

6 return to starting position and repeat

TIPS FOR PERFORMING THE EXERCISE BEST:

Do not round your lower back and control the execution of the exercise.

While performing the exercise, maintain regular and constant breathing.

11 - GLUTE BRIDGE TO THE WALL

This exercise involves all the leg muscles, tones the glutes and activates the abdominals.

STEP BY STEP EXECUTION

1 lie on the floor with your back resting on the mat

2 extend your arms at your sides

3 place your feet on the wall bending your knees at 90 degrees

4 contract your abs and glutes at the same time

5 bring your hips up

6 hold the position for a few seconds

7 return to the starting position repeat the movement

TIPS FOR PERFORMING THE EXERCISE BEST:

Check the movement and make sure you have correct execution, go down slowly.

Inhale when you are in the starting position and exhale as you begin to raise your hips.

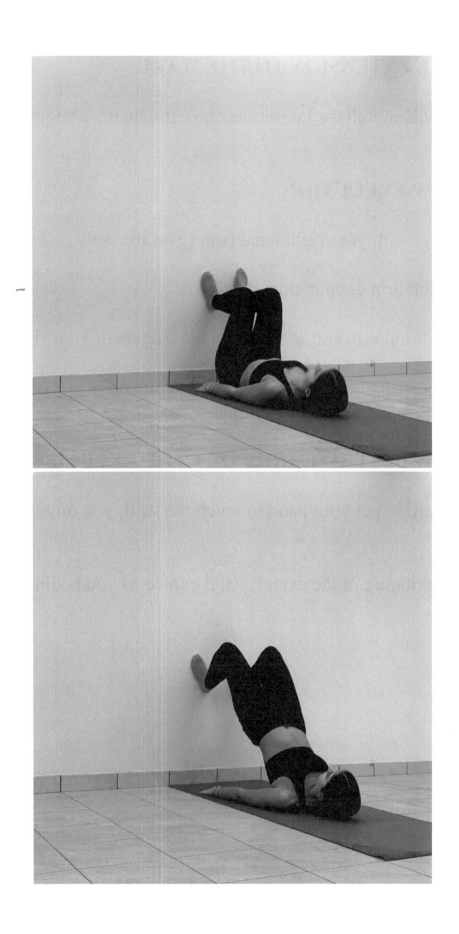

12 - LATERAL EXTENSION TO THE WALL

This exercise will stretch the latissimus and activate the oblique abdominals

STEP BY STEP EXECUTION

1 stand sideways with your right hand resting on the wall

2 extend your left arm at your side

3 now raise your left arm and try to touch the fingers of your right hand

4 return to the starting position and repeat

TIPS ON HOW BEST TO CARRY OUT THE EXERCISE:

Don't try too hard to get your hand to touch the wall, you might not succeed at first.

Inhale at the beginning of the exercise and exhale as you begin to raise your arm.

13 - SHOULDER MOBILITY WHEN STANDING

This exercise helps improve shoulder mobility and warms up the rotator cuff.

STEP BY STEP EXECUTION

1 stand up with your back and glutes leaning against the wall

2 rest your elbows on the wall forming a 90-degree angle with your arms

3 move your arms up and down trying to touch the wall with your hands

4 keep your elbows clenched to the wall throughout the entire exercise

TIPS ON HOW BEST TO CARRY OUT THE EXERCISE

Don't strain your shoulders too much, at first you probably won't be able to touch the wall with hands.

 While performing the exercise, maintain regular and constant breathing.

14 - ANGEL ON THE WALL

This exercise will improve your posture and shoulder mobility.

STEP BY STEP EXECUTION

1 stand up with your back, glutes, and head leaning against the wall

2 extend your arms at your sides

3 raise both arms without taking your hands off the wall

4 touch your hands

5 return to the starting position and start again

TIPS ON HOW BEST TO CARRY OUT THE EXERCISE

At first you can bend your arms slightly to make the movement easier.

Inhale at the beginning of the exercise and exhale as you begin to raise your arms.

15 - CHEST OPENINGS

This movement is ideal for strengthening the pectoral and deltoid muscles.

STEP BY STEP EXECUTION

1 stand up with your back, glutes, and head leaning against the wall

2 extend your arms in front of you at shoulder height

3 the palms of the hands should be resolved upwards

4 open both arms until your hands touch the wall

5 return to the starting position and touch your hands

TIPS ON HOW BEST TO CARRY OUT THE EXERCISE

keep your back, glutes, and head supported against the wall during execution e focus on the movement of your arms.

While performing the exercise, maintain regular and constant breathing.

16 - SUPERMAN POSITION

This is a comprehensive exercise that activates several muscles at once especially the glutes, abs, and stabilizers. It will improve the overall stability and balance of your body.

STEP BY STEP EXECUTION

1 rest your knees and hands on the mat

2 contract your abdominals

3 extend your right arm and left leg at the same time

4 return to the starting position and repeat on the other side

TIPS ON HOW BEST TO CARRY OUT THE EXERCISE

Keep your back straight and your abs tight to ensure you stay balanced.

Inhale at the beginning of the exercise and exhale as you begin the movement.

17 - OVERLAPPING OF THE LEGS

This exercise will improve hip mobility.

STEP BY STEP EXECUTION

1 lie on the floor with your back resting on the floor

2 place your feet on the wall bending your knees at 90 degrees

3 bring your right knee towards your chest

4 place your right foot on your left knee

5 place your right hand on your right knee and push slightly

6 place your left hand on your right foot

7 hold the position and then change legs

TIPS ON HOW BEST TO CARRY OUT THE EXERCISE

Keep your back and shoulders flat on the floor and don't push your knee too much with your hands.

While performing the exercise, maintain regular and constant breathing.

18 - FOREARM STRETCHING

This stretching exercise relaxes your forearms and lengthens your arm muscles.

STEP BY STEP EXECUTION

1 stand up with your hands resting on the wall

2 your fingers should point towards the floor

3 keep your arms straight

4 hold the position (follow the instructions in the program)

TIPS ON HOW BEST TO CARRY OUT THE EXERCISE

Do not bend your arms during the exercise.

While performing the exercise, maintain regular and constant breathing.

19 – CIRCUMDUCTION OF THE ARMS

This exercise will activate your shoulder muscles and trapezius.

STEP BY STEP EXECUTION

1 stand up with your back, glutes, and head leaning against the wall

2 extend your arms at your sides

3 put your hands together

4 raise both arms at the same time step down sideways and repeat

TIPS ON HOW BEST TO CARRY OUT THE EXERCISE

Don't hold your breath and contract your abdominals.

Inhale at the beginning of the exercise and exhale as you lower your arms.

20 - THUMB TO THE WALL

This exercise will activate your shoulder muscles and warm up your rotator cuff

STEP BY STEP EXECUTION

1 stand up with your back, glutes and head leaning against the wall

2 rest your elbows on the wall forming a 90-degree angle with your arms

3 spread your hands with palms facing up

4 touch the wall with your thumb

5 return to the starting position and repeat

TIPS ON HOW BEST TO CARRY OUT THE EXERCISE

Don't strain your shoulders too much, if you can't touch the wall with your thumb stop first.

While performing the exercise, maintain regular and constant breathing.

21 - TOUCH OPPOSITE TOES REVERSE

This exercise is great for stretching the spinal erector muscles, hamstrings, and calves.

STEP BY STEP EXECUTION

1 sit on the mat and place your feet on the wall

2 extend your legs in front of you

3 keep your arms straight at shoulder height

4 extend your right hand towards your left foot

5 touch the left foot with the fingers of the right hand

6 keep your legs as straight as possible

7 return to the starting position repeat with left arm

TIPS ON HOW BEST TO CARRY OUT THE EXERCISE

Don't push yourself too hard, especially if you're just starting out. Try to improve your performance little by little.

Inhale at the beginning of the exercise and exhale as you begin the movement.

22 - STANDING HIP OPENING

This exercise is ideal for improving hip mobility and activating the glutes.

STEP BY STEP EXECUTION

1 stand in front of the wall

2 place your hands on the wall and keep your arms straight

3 raise your right leg

4 touch your left knee with your right foot

5 spread your right leg keeping your foot on your left knee

6 return to the starting position repeat

7 the same movement with the left leg

TIPS ON HOW BEST TO CARRY OUT THE EXERCISE

Keep your abs tight and your back straight to maintain balance and stability

While performing the exercise, maintain regular and constant breathing.

23 - DOUBLE BENDING OF THE KNEES

This stretching exercise is perfect for stretching all the back muscles and activating those of the legs such as the hamstrings and flexors.

STEP BY STEP EXECUTION

1 lie down on the mat with your back resting on the floor

2 raise your legs and place your heels on the wall

3 bring your arms back keeping them straight

4 bring your knees closer to your chest

5 at the same time bring your arms towards your legs keeping them straight

6 return to the starting position and repeat

TIPS ON HOW BEST TO CARRY OUT THE EXERCISE

Control the entire range of motion and contract your abdomen as you bend your legs.

Inhale at the beginning of the exercise and exhale as you begin the movement.

24 - PENDULUM STRETCHING FOR HAMBLES

It's an excellent exercise that strengthens all the muscles of the abdomen and lengthens the femorals.

STEP BY STEP EXECUTION

1 stand up with your glutes and legs resting on the wall

2 spread your legs and keep them straight

3 cross your arms as in the photo

4 lower yourself with your arms together

5 bend first to the right and then to the left

TIPS ON HOW BEST TO CARRY OUT THE EXERCISE

Perform the movement in a slow and controlled manner.

Inhale at the beginning of the exercise and exhale as you bend to the side.

25 - STANDING DANCER

This exercise tones your glutes and strengthens your quadriceps.

STEP BY STEP EXECUTION

1 stand on tiptoe with your face facing the wall

2 place your hands on the wall

3 bend your legs slightly and bring your feet together

4 widen and close your legs dynamically

TIPS ON HOW BEST TO CARRY OUT THE EXERCISE

Control the movement and focus on the leg muscles and glutes.

Inhale before starting the movement and exhale as you spread your legs.

26 - SIDE OPENING OF THE LEGS

This exercise focuses on the glutes and stabilizing muscles

STEP BY STEP EXECUTION

1 rest your knees and hands on the mat, positioning yourself next to the wall

2 lift your right leg to the side keeping it bent

3 hold the position for a few seconds and contract your glutes well

4 return to the starting position and repeat the same movement

5 do the same with the left leg

TIPS ON HOW BEST TO CARRY OUT THE EXERCISE

Contract your abs and keep your back straight throughout the movement and find your ideal rhythm.

Inhale at the beginning of the exercise and exhale as you raise your leg.

27 - SQUAT WITH DYNAMIC CHANGE

This exercise strengthens all the leg muscles and tones the glutes.

STEP BY STEP EXECUTION

1 stand upright with your face facing the wall

2 place your hands on the wall and keep your arms semi-stretched

3 do a squat

4 never take your hands off the wall

5 change your foot position dynamically (as shown in the video) and repeat the squat

6 reposition your feet and repeat the movement below

TIPS ON HOW BEST TO CARRY OUT THE EXERCISE

At the beginning, don't bend your knees too much and help yourself a lot with your hands.

Inhale as you go down and exhale as you go up.

28 - ELEVATED GLUTE BRIDGE WITH KNEE OPENING

This more advanced exercise aims to improve hip mobility and tone the glutes. It also strengthens your abdominals and activates your hamstrings.

STEP BY STEP EXECUTION

1 lie on the floor with your back resting on the mat

2 extend your arms at your sides and face your palms towards the floor

3 place your feet on the wall bending your knees at 90 degrees

4 contract your abs and glutes

5 bring your hips up

6 spread your knees while keeping your abdomen and glutes contracted

7 return to the starting position repeat the movement

TIPS ON HOW BEST TO CARRY OUT THE EXERCISE

Control the movement throughout the execution and descend slowly.

Inhale at the beginning of the exercise and exhale as you begin to raise your hips.

29 - PLANK + DORSAL STRETCH

This is a more advanced exercise than the others that will activate all your muscles of the abdomen and will stretch the lower back.

STEP BY STEP EXECUTION

1 place your feet on the wall, your knees, and hands on the mat

2 get into a plank position with your arms straight and contract your abdomen

3 bend your legs and place your knees on the floor

4 stretch your back well

5 return to the starting position and repeat

TIPS ON HOW BEST TO CARRY OUT THE EXERCISE

Keep your back straight throughout the range of motion and stretch as far as possible when bending your knees.

Inhale at the beginning of the exercise and exhale as you stretch.

30 - LEG RAISE + WALL KICK BACK

This exercise is great for toning your glutes and warming up your hip joints.

STEP BY STEP EXECUTION

1 stand upright with your face facing the wall

2 place your palms on the wall

3 raise your right knee towards your chest

4 extend your right leg backwards, contracting your glutes

5 repeat the movement and then change legs

TIPS ON HOW BEST TO CARRY OUT THE EXERCISE

Keep your arms outstretched throughout the movement and perform the exercise in a slow, controlled manner.

Inhale as you lift your knee and exhale as you straighten your leg backwards.

31 - UNILATERAL WALL BRIDGE

This exercise is perfect for toning your glutes, improving hip mobility, and strengthening your hamstrings

STEP BY STEP EXECUTION

1 lie down with your back resting on the mat

2 place your feet on the wall and bend your knees

3 extend your arms at your sides with palms facing down

4 contract your glutes and raise your hips by lifting one leg off the wall

5 hold your position

6 go back down and repeat the movement

TIPS ON HOW BEST TO CARRY OUT THE EXERCISE

Contract your abs well to keep your lower back straight.
Never take your arms off the floor, they help you maintain balance.

Inhale as you begin the exercise and exhale as you contract your glutes and raise your hips.

32 - TRICEPS WALL PUSH-UPS

In this exercise, the triceps and stabilizing muscles will be particularly involved.

STEP BY STEP EXECUTION

1 stand upright with your face facing the wall

2 place your palms on the wall and stretch your arms

3 bend your arms and touch the wall with your elbows bringing your face closer to the wall

4 find your rhythm and repeat the movement

TIPS ON HOW BEST TO CARRY OUT THE EXERCISE

At the beginning don't stand too far from the wall and become familiar with the movement, over time you can increase the difficulty by increasing the distance of your feet from the wall.

Inhale as you bend your elbows and exhale as you return to the position and extend your arms

33 - COBRA BENDING

This stretching exercise will activate your triceps and lengthen your lower back.

STEP BY STEP EXECUTION

1 lie on your stomach on the mat

2 bend your legs and place your feet on the wall

3 place your hands near your hips and push up until you relax your arms completely

4 return to starting position and repeat

TIPS ON HOW BEST TO CARRY OUT THE EXERCISE

Don't put too much strain on your lower back and perform the movement slowly and in a controlled manner to avoid back pain.

Inhale when you are lying down and exhale when you extend your arms.

34 – WALL KICK BACK

Excellent exercise to stimulate and tone the glutes

STEP BY STEP EXECUTION

1 stand upright with your face facing the wall

2 place your palms on the wall and stretch your arms

3 bring your right leg backwards keeping it straight

4 hold the position for a few seconds

5 return to starting position and repeat

TIPS ON HOW BEST TO CARRY OUT THE EXERCISE

Keep your glutes tight throughout the exercise and control the movement.

Inhale at the beginning of the exercise and exhale as you bring your leg back.

35 - ALTERNATE LEG RAISE

This exercise is ideal for stretching your hamstrings and improving mobility.

STEP BY STEP EXECUTION

1 lie down with your back resting on the mat

2 stretch your legs and place your heels on the wall

3 bring your right knee towards your chest

4 try not to bend your leg too much

5 return to the starting position and repeat the exercise

TRICKS AND TIPS

Extend your arms at your sides to maintain balance and stability.

Inhale at the beginning of the exercise and exhale as you bring your knee towards your chest.

36 - DYNAMIC PLANK

This more advanced version of the plank is great for continuous stimulation the abdominals throughout the exercise.

STEP BY STEP EXECUTION

1 get into a plank position with your arms outstretched and your head facing the wall

2 contract your abs and take one hand off the floor and touch the wall

3 return to the starting position and do the same with the other hand

4 return to the starting position and repeat

TIPS ON HOW BEST TO CARRY OUT THE EXERCISE

Keep your back straight throughout the range of motion and find your ideal rhythm while maintaining balance and stability.

While performing the exercise, maintain regular and constant breathing.

37 - SQUAT WITH STATIC BLOCK

This exercise strengthens all the leg muscles and tones the glutes.

STEP BY STEP EXECUTION

1 stand upright with your face facing the wall

2 place your hands on the wall and keep your arms semi-stretched

3 do a squat without taking your hands off the wall

4 hold the position for a few seconds

5 go up pushing hard on the quadriceps

TIPS ON HOW BEST TO CARRY OUT THE EXERCISE

At the beginning, don't bend your knees too much and Help yourself a lot with your hands.

Inhale as you go down and exhale as you go up.

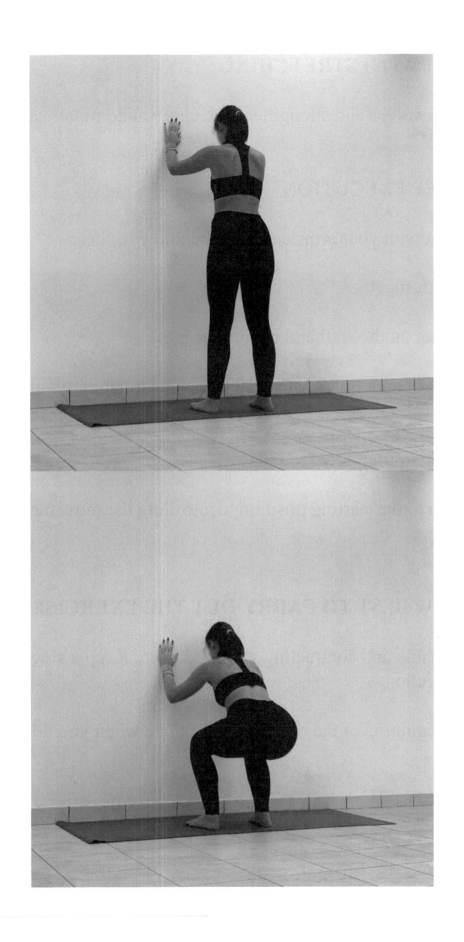

38 - CRUNCH WITH STRETCHING

This exercise involves and strengthens the entire abdominal wall.

STEP BY STEP EXECUTION

1 lie on the mat with your arms extended behind your head

2 put your hands together

3 place your feet on the wall and bend your legs

4 do a crunch by contracting your abdomen and stretching your arms towards the wall

5 hold the position for a few seconds

6 slowly return to the starting position, controlling the movement

TIPS ON HOW BEST TO CARRY OUT THE EXERCISE

Focus on breathing and contracting your abdomen. Keep a slow and controlled execution.

Inhale at the beginning of the exercise and exhale when you do the crunch.

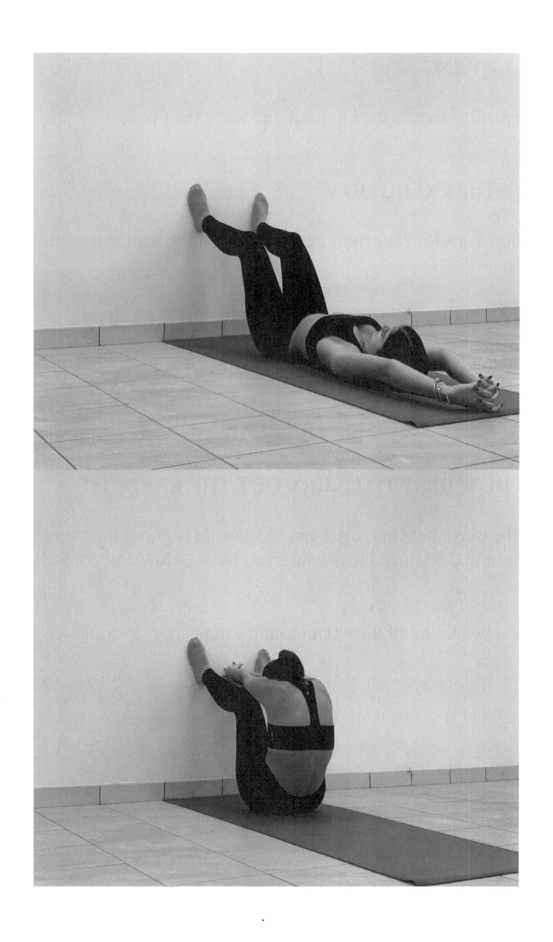

39 - WALL SWING

This movement activates the hip joint and tones the glutes

STEP BY STEP EXECUTION

1 stand sideways with your right hand resting on the wall and your left hand on your hip

2 extend your left leg in front of you, bending your knee slightly

3 now stretch it backwards by contracting your glutes

4 repeat the movement and then change legs

TIPS ON HOW BEST TO CARRY OUT THE EXERCISE

Focus on the movement and maintain balance throughout the exercise. Contract your abdomen and make sure you have a slow and controlled execution.

Inhale at the beginning of the exercise and exhale as you straighten your leg.

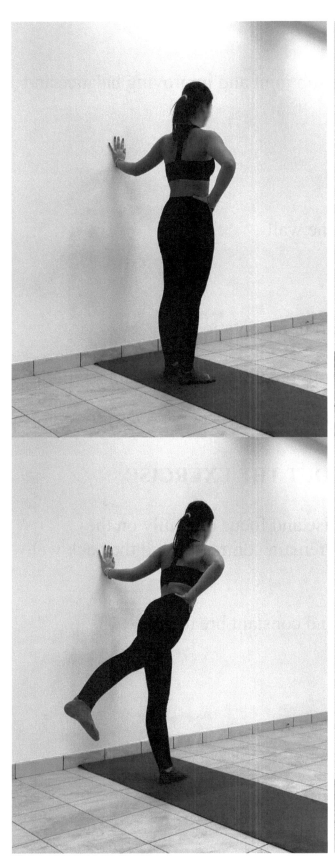

40 – LEGS ROTATION

This exercise is ideal for activating the hip joint and improving balance and stability

STEP BY STEP EXECUTION

1 stand up and lean your back against the wall

2 place your hands on your hips

3 extend your right leg forward and start doing rotations

4 once you have completed the number of repetitions, do the same with the left leg

TIPS ON HOW BEST TO CARRY OUT THE EXERCISE

Maintain balance throughout the exercise and focus carefully on the movement. The abdomen must always remain contracted and the back well supported against the wall.

During the exercise, maintain regular and constant breathing.

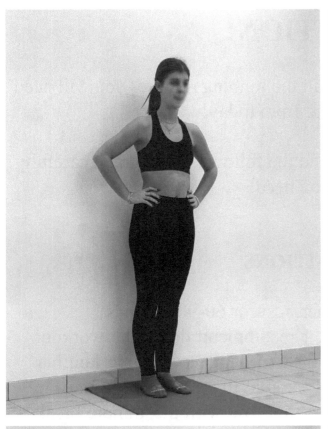 

ATTENTION!

On the following pages you will find all the training routines you will need to perform for the next 30 days starting from today!

Before starting, I kindly ask you to read the following paragraph carefully so that you have all the information you need!

RECOVERY TIMES AND REPETITIONS

- Between one exercise and another, rest for 60-90 seconds
- If you are a complete beginner, I recommend doing the workout routine only once! Over time you will begin to become familiar with the exercises and you will be able to start carrying out the same proposed routine 2-3 times in a row with a 5-minute break between one routine and another.

LISTEN TO YOUR BODY!

I advise you to listen to your body and, if necessary, to modify your training based on any physical problems that prevent you from carrying out certain exercises or movements in maximum safety! The proposed routines are designed to offer you different stimuli every day so as to train all the muscles in your body and keep your motivation and curiosity always high. However, it is highly recommended to customize the workouts according to your starting level and the feelings you will have during the workout.

ARE YOU READY? LET'S GO!

NAME OF THE EXERCISE	PAGE	REPETITIONS/DURATION
	DAY 1	
FORWARD BEND FROM A SEATED POSITION (EXERCISE 1)	1	12 REPETITIONS
CALF STRETCH (EXERCISE 8)	15	5 REPETITIONS PER LEG
CHEST OPENINGS (EXERCISE 15)	29	20 REPETITIONS
STANDING HIP OPENING (EXERCISE 22)	43	10 REPETITIONS PER LEG
PLANK + DORSAL STRETCH (EXERCISE 29)	57	15 REPETITIONS
DYNAMIC PLANK (EXERCISE 36)	71	10 REPETITIONS PER SIDE
	DAY 2	
KNEES TO CHEST WHEN SEATED (EXERCISE 2)	3	10 REPETITIONS PER LEG
ONE-SIDED WALL SLIDING (EXERCISE 9)	17	15 REPETITIONS PER SIDE
SUPERMAN POSITION (EXERCISE 16)	31	10 REPETITIONS PER SIDE
DOUBLE BENDING OF THE KNEES (EXERCISE 23)	45	12 REPETITIONS
LEG RAISE + WALL KICK BACK (EXERCISE 40)	59	10 REPETITIONS PER SIDE
SQUAT WITH STATIC BLOCK (EXERCISE 37)	73	10 REPETITIONS

NAME OF THE EXERCISE	PAGE	REPETITIONS/DURATION
	DAY 3	
ARMS MOBILITY WHEN SEATED (EXERCISE 3)	5	12 REPETITIONS
LYING DOWN WALK (EXERCISE 10)	19	12 REPETITIONS
OVERLAPPING OF THE LEGS (EXERCISE 17)	33	12 REPETITIONS PER SIDE
PENDULUM STRETCHING FOR HAMBLES (EXERCISE 24)	47	10 REPETITIONS PER SIDE
UNILATERAL WALL BRIDGE (EXERCISE 31)	61	10 REPETITIONS PER SIDE
CRUNCH WITH STRETCHING (EXERCISE 38)	75	12 REPETITIONS
	DAY 4	
SINGLE-LEG LATERAL SWING (EXERCISE 6)	11	15 REPETITIONS PER LEG
GLUTE BRIDGE TO THE WALL (EXERCISE 11)	21	12 REPETITIONS
FOREARM STRETCHING (EXERCISE 18)	35	30 SECONDS
STANDING DANCER (EXERCISE 25)	49	12 REPETITIONS
TRICEPS WALL PUSH-UPS (EXERCISE 32)	63	15 REPETITIONS
WALL SWING (EXERCISE 39)	77	12 REPETITIONS PER LEG

NAME OF THE EXERCISE	PAGE	REPETITIONS/DURATION
	DAY 5	
ARM STRETCHING (EXERCISE 5)	9	12 REPETITIONS PER SIDE
LATERAL EXTENSION TO THE WALL (EXERCISE 12)	23	10 REPETITIONS PER SIDE
CIRCUMDUCTION OF THE ARMS (EXERCISE 19)	37	15 REPETITIONS
SIDE OPENING OF THE LEGS (EXERCISE 26)	51	10 REPETITIONS PER SIDE
COBRA BENDING (EXERCISE 33)	65	12 REPETITIONS
LEGS ROTATION (EXERCISE 40)	79	15 REPETITIONS PER LEG
	DAY 6	
SINGLE-LEG LATERAL SWING (EXERCISE 6)	11	15 REPETITIONS PER LEG
STANDING DANCER (EXERCISE 25)	49	12 REPETITIONS
THUMB TO THE WALL (EXERCISE 20)	39	20 REPETITIONS
SQUAT WITH DYNAMIC CHANGE (EXERCISE 27)	53	10 REPETITIONS
WALL KICK BACK (EXERCISE 34)	67	15 REPETITIONS PER LEG
TOUCH OPPOSITE TOES REVERSE (EXERCISE 21)	41	12 REPETITIONS PER SIDE

NAME OF THE EXERCISE	PAGE	REPETITIONS/DURATION
	DAY 7	
STRETCHING INVERSE FROG POSITION (EXERCISE 7)	13	30 SECONDS
ANGEL ON THE WALL (EXERCISE 14)	27	15 REPETITIONS
TOUCH OPPOSITE TOES REVERSE (EXERCISE 21)	41	12 REPETITIONS PER SIDE
ELEVATED GLUTE BRIDGE WITH KNEE OPENING (EXERCISE 28)	55	10 REPETITIONS
ALTERNATE LEG RAISE (EXERCISE 35)	69	12 REPETITIONS PER LEG
	DAY 8	
WALL KICK BACK (EXERCISE 34)	67	15 REPETITIONS PER LEG
STRETCHING INVERSE FROG POSITION (EXERCISE 7)	13	30 SECONDS
THUMB TO THE WALL (EXERCISE 20)	39	20 REPETITIONS
SQUAT WITH DYNAMIC CHANGE (EXERCISE 27)	53	10 REPETITIONS
WALL SWING (EXERCISE 39)	77	12 REPETITIONS PER LEG
ANGEL ON THE WALL (EXERCISE 14)	27	15 REPETITIONS

NAME OF THE EXERCISE	PAGE	REPETITIONS/DURATION
	DAY 9	
KNEES TO CHEST WHEN SEATED (EXERCISE 2)	3	10 REPETITIONS PER LEG
STRETCHING INVERSE FROG POSITION (EXERCISE 7)	13	30 SECONDS
LATERAL EXTENSION TO THE WALL (EXERCISE 12)	23	10 REPETITIONS PER SIDE
OVERLAPPING OF THE LEGS (EXERCISE 17)	33	12 REPETITIONS PER SIDE
STANDING HIP OPENING (EXERCISE 22)	43	10 REPETITIONS PER LEG
SQUAT WITH DYNAMIC CHANGE (EXERCISE 27)	53	10 REPETITIONS
TRICEPS WALL PUSH-UPS (EXERCISE 32)	63	15 REPETITIONS
	DAY 10	
ARMS MOBILITY WHEN SEATED (EXERCISE 3)	5	12 REPETITIONS
CALF STRETCH (EXERCISE 8)	15	5 REPETITIONS PER LEG
STANDING DANCER (EXERCISE 25)	49	12 REPETITIONS
FOREARM STRETCHING (EXERCISE 18)	35	30 SECONDS
DOUBLE BENDING OF THE KNEES (EXERCISE 23)	45	12 REPETITIONS
ELEVATED GLUTE BRIDGE WITH KNEE OPENING (EXERCISE 28)	55	10 REPETITIONS
COBRA BENDING (EXERCISE 33)	65	12 REPETITIONS
CRUNCH WITH STRETCHING (EXERCISE 38)	75	12 REPETITIONS

NAME OF THE EXERCISE	PAGE	REPETITIONS/DURATION
	DAY 11	
SINGLE LEG BENDING (EXERCISE 4)	7	15 REPETITIONS PER LEG
ONE-SIDED WALL SLIDING (EXERCISE 9)	17	15 REPETITIONS PER SIDE
ANGEL ON THE WALL (EXERCISE 14)	27	15 REPETITIONS
CIRCUMDUCTION OF THE ARMS (EXERCISE 19)	37	15 REPETITIONS
PENDULUM STRETCHING FOR HAMBLES (EXERCISE 24)	47	10 REPETITIONS PER SIDE
PLANK + DORSAL STRETCH (EXERCISE 29)	57	15 REPETITIONS
WALL KICK BACK (EXERCISE 34)	67	15 REPETITIONS PER LEG
WALL SWING (EXERCISE 39)	77	12 REPETITIONS PER LEG
	DAY 12	
ARM STRETCHING (EX. 5)	9	12 REPETITIONS PER SIDE
LYING DOWN WALK (EXERCISE 10)	19	12 REPETITIONS PER LEG
CHEST OPENINGS (EX.15)	29	20 REPETITIONS
THUMB TO THE WALL (EXERCISE 20)	39	20 REPETITIONS
STANDING DANCER (EXERCISE 25)	49	12 REPETITIONS
LEG RAISE + WALL KICK BACK (EXERCISE 30)	59	10 REPETITIONS PER SIDE
ALTERNATE LEG RAISE (EXERCISE 35)	69	12 REPETITIONS PER LEG
LEGS ROTATION (EXERCISE 40)	79	15 REPETITIONS PER LEG

NAME OF THE EXERCISE	PAGE	REPETITIONS/DURATION
	DAY 13	
SINGLE-LEG LATERAL SWING (EXERCISE 6)	11	15 REPETITIONS PER LEG
GLUTE BRIDGE TO THE WALL (EXERCISE 11)	21	12 REPETITIONS
SUPERMAN POSITION (EXERCISE 16)	31	10 REPETITIONS PER SIDE
TOUCH OPPOSITE TOES REVERSE (EXERCISE 21)	41	12 REPETITIONS PER SIDE
SIDE OPENING OF THE LEGS (EXERCISE 26)	51	10 REPETITIONS PER SIDE
UNILATERAL WALL BRIDGE (EXERCISE 31)	61	10 REPETITIONS PER SIDE
	DAY 14	
FORWARD BEND FROM A SEATED POSITION (EXERCISE 1)	1	12 REPETITIONS
STRETCHING INVERSE FROG POSITION (EXERCISE 7)	13	30 SECONDS
STANDING DANCER (EXERCISE 25)	49	12 REPETITIONS
CIRCUMDUCTION OF THE ARMS (EXERCISE 19)	37	15 REPETITIONS
STANDING DANCER (EXERCISE 25)	49	12 REPETITIONS
UNILATERAL WALL BRIDGE (EXERCISE 31)	61	10 REPETITIONS PER SIDE
SQUAT WITH STATIC BLOCK (EXERCISE 37)	73	10 REPETITIONS

NAME OF THE EXERCISE	PAGE	REPETITIONS/DURATION
	DAY 15	
FORWARD BEND FROM A SEATED POSITION (EXERCISE 1)	1	12 REPETITIONS
ONE-SIDED WALL SLIDING (EXERCISE 9)	17	15 REPETITIONS PER SIDE
OVERLAPPING OF THE LEGS (EXERCISE 17)	33	12 REPETITIONS PER SIDE
STANDING DANCER (EXERCISE 25)	49	12 REPETITIONS
COBRA BENDING (EXERCISE 33)	65	12 REPETITIONS
WALL SWING (EXERCISE 39)	77	12 REPETITIONS PER LEG
	DAY 16	
KNEES TO CHEST WHEN SEATED (EXERCISE 2)	3	10 REPETITIONS PER LEG
LYING DOWN WALK (EXERCISE 10)	19	12 REPETITIONS PER LEG
FOREARM STRETCHING (EXERCISE 18)	35	30 SECONDS
SIDE OPENING OF THE LEGS (EXERCISE 26)	51	10 REPETITIONS PER SIDE
WALL KICK BACK (EXERCISE 34)	67	15 REPETITIONS PER LEG
LEGS ROTATION (EXERCISE 40)	79	15 REPETITIONS PER LEG

NAME OF THE EXERCISE	PAGE	REPETITIONS/DURATION
	DAY 17	
ARMS MOBILITY WHEN SEATED (EXERCISE 3)	5	12 REPETITIONS
GLUTE BRIDGE TO THE WALL (EXERCISE 11)	21	12 REPETITIONS
CIRCUMDUCTION OF THE ARMS (EXERCISE 19)	37	15 REPETITIONS
SQUAT WITH DYNAMIC CHANGE (EXERCISE 27)	53	10 REPETITIONS
ALTERNATE LEG RAISE (EXERCISE 35)	69	12 REPETITIONS PER LEG
CALF STRETCH (EXERCISE 8)	15	5 REPETITIONS PER LEG
	DAY 18	
SINGLE LEG BENDING (EXERCISE 4)	7	15 REPETITIONS PER LEG
LATERAL EXTENSION TO THE WALL (EXERCISE 12)	23	10 REPETITIONS PER SIDE
THUMB TO THE WALL (EXERCISE 20)	39	20 REPETITIONS
ELEVATED GLUTE BRIDGE WITH KNEE OPENING (EXERCISE 28)	55	10 REPETITIONS
DYNAMIC PLANK (EXERCISE 36)	71	10 REPETITIONS PER SIDE
STRETCHING INVERSE FROG POSITION (EXERCISE 7)	13	30 SECONDS

NAME OF THE EXERCISE	PAGE	REPETITIONS/DURATION
	DAY 19	
ARM STRETCHING (EXERCISE 5)	9	12 REPETITIONS PER SIDE
STANDING DANCER (EXERCISE 25)	49	12 REPETITIONS
TOUCH OPPOSITE TOES REVERSE (EXERCISE 21)	41	12 REPETITIONS PER SIDE
PLANK + DORSAL STRETCH (EXERCISE 29)	57	15 REPETITIONS
SQUAT WITH STATIC BLOCK (EXERCISE 37)	73	10 REPETITIONS
SINGLE-LEG LATERAL SWING (EXERCISE 6)	11	15 REPETITIONS PER LEG
	DAY 20	
SINGLE-LEG LATERAL SWING (EXERCISE 6)	11	15 REPETITIONS PER LEG
ANGEL ON THE WALL (EXERCISE 14)	27	15 REPETITIONS
STANDING HIP OPENING (EXERCISE 22)	43	10 REPETITIONS PER LEG
LEG RAISE + WALL KICK BACK (EXERCISE 30)	59	10 REPETITIONS PER SIDE
CRUNCH WITH STRETCHING (EXERCISE 38)	75	12 REPETITIONS
CHEST OPENINGS (EXERCISE 15)	29	20 REPETITIONS

NAME OF THE EXERCISE	PAGE	REPETITIONS/DURATION
	DAY 21	
FORWARD BEND FROM A SEATED POSITION (EXERCISE 1)	1	12 REPETITIONS
ANGEL ON THE WALL (EXERCISE 14)	27	15 REPETITIONS
TOUCH OPPOSITE TOES REVERSE (EXERCISE 21)	41	12 REPETITIONS PER SIDE
TRICEPS WALL PUSH-UPS (EXERCISE 32)	63	15 REPETITIONS
ALTERNATE LEG RAISE (EXERCISE 35)	69	12 REPETITIONS PER LEG
LEGS ROTATION (EXERCISE 40)	79	15 REPETITIONS PER LEG
	DAY 22	
KNEES TO CHEST WHEN SEATED (EXERCISE 2)	3	10 REPETITIONS
CHEST OPENINGS (EXERCISE 15)	29	20 REPETITIONS
STANDING HIP OPENING (EXERCISE 22)	43	10 REPETITIONS PER LEG
COBRA BENDING (EXERCISE 33)	65	12 REPETITIONS
DYNAMIC PLANK (EXERCISE 36)	71	10 REPETITIONS PER SIDE
WALL SWING (EXERCISE 39)	77	12 REPETITIONS PER LEG

NAME OF THE EXERCISE	PAGE	REPETITIONS/DURATION
	DAY 23	
ARMS MOBILITY WHEN SEATED (EXERCISE 3)	5	12 REPETITIONS
SUPERMAN POSITION (EXERCISE 16)	31	10 REPETITIONS PER SIDE
DOUBLE BENDING OF THE KNEES (EXERCISE 23)	45	12 REPETITIONS
WALL KICK BACK (EXERCISE 34)	67	15 REPETITIONS PER LEG
SQUAT WITH STATIC BLOCK (EXERCISE 37)	73	10 REPETITIONS
	DAY 24	
SINGLE LEG BENDING (EXERCISE 4)	7	15 REPETITIONS PER LEG
OVERLAPPING OF THE LEGS (EXERCISE 17)	33	12 REPETITIONS PER SIDE
PENDULUM STRETCHING FOR HAMBLES (EXERCISE 24)	47	10 REPETITIONS PER SIDE
ALTERNATE LEG RAISE (EXERCISE 35)	69	12 REPETITIONS PER LEG
CRUNCH WITH STRETCHING (EXERCISE 38)	75	12 REPETITIONS

NAME OF THE EXERCISE	PAGE	REPETITIONS/DURATION
	DAY 25	
ARM STRETCHING (EXERCISE 5)	9	12 REPETITIONS PER SIDE
FOREARM STRETCHING (EXERCISE 18)	35	30 SECONDS
STANDING DANCER (EXERCISE 25)	49	12 REPETITIONS
DYNAMIC PLANK (EXERCISE 36)	71	10 REPETITIONS PER SIDE
LEGS ROTATION (EXERCISE 40)	79	15 REPETITIONS PER LEG
	DAY 26	
SINGLE-LEG LATERAL SWING (EXERCISE 6)	11	15 REPETITIONS PER LEG
CIRCUMDUCTION OF THE ARMS (EXERCISE 19)	37	15 REPETITIONS
SIDE OPENING OF THE LEGS (EXERCISE 26)	51	10 REPETITIONS PER SIDE
SQUAT WITH STATIC BLOCK (EXERCISE 37)	73	10 REPETITIONS
LEGS ROTATION (EXERCISE 40)	79	15 REPETITIONS PER LEG

NAME OF THE EXERCISE	PAGE	REPETITIONS/DURATION
	DAY 27	
STRETCHING INVERSE FROG POSITION (EXERCISE 7)	13	30 SECONDS
SUPERMAN POSITION (EXERCISE 16)	31	10 REPETITIONS PER SIDE
STANDING DANCER (EXERCISE 25)	49	12 REPETITIONS
WALL KICK BACK (EXERCISE 34)	67	15 REPETITIONS PER LEG
WALL SWING (EXERCISE 39)	77	12 REPETITIONS PER LEG
	DAY 28	
CALF STRETCH (EXERCISE 8)	15	5 REPETITIONS PER LEG
OVERLAPPING OF THE LEGS (EXERCISE 17)	33	12 REPETITIONS PER SIDE
SIDE OPENING OF THE LEGS (EXERCISE 26)	51	10 REPETITIONS PER SIDE
ALTERNATE LEG RAISE (EXERCISE 35)	69	12 REPETITIONS PER LEG
LEGS ROTATION (EXERCISE 40)	79	15 REPETITIONS PER LEG

NAME OF THE EXERCISE	PAGE	REPETITIONS/DURATION
	DAY 29	
ONE-SIDED WALL SLIDING (EXERCISE 9)	17	15 REPETITIONS PER SIDE
FOREARM STRETCHING (EXERCISE 18)	35	30 SECONDS
SQUAT WITH DYNAMIC CHANGE (EXERCISE 27)	53	10 REPETITIONS
DYNAMIC PLANK (EXERCISE 36)	71	10 REPETITIONS PER SIDE
SQUAT WITH STATIC BLOCK (EXERCISE 37)	73	10 REPETITIONS
	DAY 30	
LYING DOWN WALK (EXERCISE 10)	19	12 REPETITIONS PER LEG
CIRCUMDUCTION OF THE ARMS (EXERCISE 19)	37	15 REPETITIONS
ELEVATED GLUTE BRIDGE WITH KNEE OPENING (EXERCISE 28)	55	10 REPETITIONS
PLANK + DORSAL STRETCH (EXERCISE 29)	57	15 REPETITIONS
CRUNCH WITH STRETCHING (EXERCISE 38)	75	12 REPETITIONS

Made in United States
Troutdale, OR
05/03/2024

19614639R00064